Thinking Critically:
Social Media

Bradley Steffens

San Diego, CA

© 2023 ReferencePoint Press, Inc.
Printed in the United States

For more information, contact:
ReferencePoint Press, Inc.
PO Box 27779
San Diego, CA 92198
www.ReferencePointPress.com

ALL RIGHTS RESERVED.
No part of this work covered by the copyright hereon may be reproduced or used in any form or by any means—graphic, electronic, or mechanical, including photocopying, recording, taping, web distribution, or information storage retrieval systems—without the written permission of the publisher.

LIBRARY OF CONGRESS CATALOGING-IN-PUBLICATION DATA

Names: Steffens, Bradley, 1955- author.
Title: Thinking critically: social media / by Bradley Steffens.
Other titles: Social media
Description: San Diego, CA : ReferencePoint Press, Inc., 2023. | Series: Thinking critically | Includes bibliographical references and index.
Identifiers: LCCN 2022039160 (print) | LCCN 2022039161 (ebook) | ISBN 9781678204648 (library binding) | ISBN 9781678204655 (ebook)
Subjects: LCSH: Social media--Psychological aspects--Juvenile literature. | Internet--Social aspects--Juvenile literature. | Social media--Moral and ethical aspects--Juvenile literature. | Electronic information resource literacy--Juvenile literature.
Classification: LCC HM742 .S836 2023 (print) | LCC HM742 (ebook) | DDC 302.23/1--dc23/eng/20220908
LC record available at https://lccn.loc.gov/2022039160
LC ebook record available at https://lccn.loc.gov/2022039161

Contents

Foreword	4
Overview: A Challenge to Civil Society	6
Chapter One: Is Social Media Use Harmful to Youth Mental Health?	
The Debate at a Glance	12
Social Media Use Harms Mental Health in Young People	13
Social Media Use Benefits Mental Health in Young People	19
Chapter Two: Should Social Media Companies Regulate Speech?	
The Debate at a Glance	25
Social Media Companies Should Regulate Speech	26
Social Media Companies Should Not Regulate Free Speech	32
Chapter Three: Is Social Media Addictive?	
The Debate at a Glance	38
Social Media Is Addictive	39
Social Media Is Not Addictive	44
Source Notes	50
Social Media Facts	53
Related Organizations and Websites	55
For Further Research	57
Index	59
Picture Credits	63
About the Author	64

Foreword

"Literacy is the most basic currency of the knowledge economy we're living in today." Barack Obama (at the time a senator from Illinois) spoke these words during a 2005 speech before the American Library Association. One question raised by this statement is: What does it mean to be a literate person in the twenty-first century?

E.D. Hirsch Jr., author of *Cultural Literacy: What Every American Needs to Know*, answers the question this way: "To be culturally literate is to possess the basic information needed to thrive in the modern world. The breadth of the information is great, extending over the major domains of human activity from sports to science."

But literacy in the twenty-first century goes beyond the accumulation of knowledge gained through study and experience and expanded over time. Now more than ever literacy requires the ability to sift through and evaluate vast amounts of information and, as the authors of the Common Core State Standards state, to "demonstrate the cogent reasoning and use of evidence that is essential to both private deliberation and responsible citizenship in a democratic republic."

The Thinking Critically series challenges students to become discerning readers, to think independently, and to engage and develop their skills as critical thinkers. Through a narrative-driven, pro/con format, the series introduces students to the complex issues that dominate public discourse—topics such as gun control and violence, social networking, and medical marijuana. All chapters revolve around a single, pointed question such as Can Stronger Gun Control Measures Prevent Mass Shootings?, or Does Social Networking Benefit Society?, or Should Medical Marijuana Be Legalized? This inquiry-based approach introduces student researchers to core issues and concerns on a given topic. Each chapter includes one part that argues the affirmative and one part that argues the negative—all written by a single author. With the single-author format the predominant arguments for and against an issue can be synthesized into clear, accessible discussions supported by details and evidence including relevant facts, direct quotes, current examples, and statistical illustrations. All volumes include focus questions to guide students as they read each pro/con discussion, a list of key facts, and an annotated list of related organizations and websites for conducting further research.

The authors of the Common Core State Standards have set out the particular qualities that a literate person in the twenty-first century must have. These include the ability to think independently, establish a base of knowledge across a wide range of subjects, engage in open-minded but discerning reading and listening, know how to use and evaluate evidence, and appreciate and understand diverse perspectives. The new Thinking Critically series supports these goals by providing a solid introduction to the study of pro/con issues.

A Challenge to Civil Society

On May 14, 2022, eighteen-year-old Payton Gendron walked into a Tops Friendly Markets store on the east side of Buffalo, New York, wearing body armor and armed with a military-style rifle. Gendron was not there to buy anything. He was there to kill. According to investigators, Gendron opened fire on shoppers and store employees with his semiautomatic rifle while live-streaming the attack on Twitch, a social media website popular with gamers. Minutes later, ten people lay dead. Another three were wounded.

The shooter did not know any of his victims. He did not attack them because of anything they had said or done. He targeted them because of their skin color. Gendron is White, while eleven of the thirteen people he shot—including all ten who lost their lives—were Black.

Encountering a Racist Ideology

According to a 180-page manifesto Gendron posted online, he subscribed to the White replacement theory, a racist ideology that maintains that non-White minorities are replacing White majorities in the United States, Europe, and other mostly White countries with the purpose of eliminating White culture. According to Gendron's manifesto, his shooting spree was part of a global White supremacist movement to eliminate as many non-White people as possible.

The movement Gendron identifies with takes its name and some of its tenets from a 2011 book entitled *Le Grand Rem-*

placement (The great replacement) by French author Renaud Camus. But Gendron never read this book. Instead, he learned about its ideas by reading White supremacist rants and memes posted on social media websites. "I started browsing 4chan in May 2020 after extreme boredom, remember this was during the outbreak of covid," Gendron wrote in his manifesto. "There I learned through infographics, [posts], and memes that the White race is dying out."[1]

Three days after the Tops supermarket massacre, President Joe Biden visited Buffalo to honor the dead and speak out against the racist ideology that motivated the shooter. The president acknowledged the role social media played in bringing racist ideology into Gendron's life. "You can't prevent people from being radicalized to violence, but we can address the relentless exploitation of the Internet to recruit and mobilize terrorism,"[2] Biden said.

Sadly, Gendron's rampage was not the first mass shooting stoked by online hate speech. In 2019 twenty-one-year-old Patrick Crusius opened fire on a Walmart in El Paso, Texas, killing twenty-two people and injuring twenty-six. Like Gendron, Crusius posted a racist screed online before committing his mass murder. In his rant, Crusius stated that his actions were "a response to the Hispanic invasion of Texas" and the "ethnic displacement" of Whites. In 2015 twenty-two-year-old Dylann Roof killed nine Black parishioners in South Carolina. At Roof's trial, Roof's attorney, David Bruck, told the jury how the killer came to hold his racist views: "Every bit of motivation came from things he saw on the internet. That's it. . . . He is simply regurgitating, in whole paragraphs, slogans and facts—bits and pieces of facts that he downloaded from the internet directly into his brain."[3]

> "You can't prevent people from being radicalized to violence, but we can address the relentless exploitation of the Internet to recruit and mobilize terrorism."[2]
>
> —Joe Biden, president of the United States

> "Every bit of motivation came from things he saw on the internet."[3]
>
> —David Bruck, attorney for mass shooter Dylann Roof

Three days after the 2022 Tops supermarket massacre, President Joe Biden and First Lady Jill Biden pay their respects at a makeshift memorial for the victims. In his remarks, the president spoke about the role of social media in spreading racist and violent ideologies and encouraging real-world violence.

Spreading Fear Online

Mass shootings are the most heinous hate crimes, but they are far from the only ones. For every mass shooting, thousands of lesser hate crimes are committed. White supremacists burn crosses to terrorize Blacks. Religious bigots deface synagogues and mosques with graffiti. Bullies yell at or even beat innocent people because of their race, ethnicity, religion, gender, sexual preference, or even disability. Many of these hate crimes are memorialized on social media to spread the fear to others.

Even more often, bigots and bullies do not commit physical crimes but instead use social media to harass and intimidate others, posting hate-filled messages, memes, and photos in the feeds or comments of the intended victims. In a 2020 Pew Research Center survey, 41 percent of US adults said they had personally experienced online harassment at some point in their lives, with 64 percent of those under age thirty saying they had been harassed online. Meanwhile, another Pew Research Center study found that 59 percent of US teens reported having been bullied or harassed online.

Medical Disinformation

Hate speech, bullying, and harassment are the most hurtful forms of communication on social media because the verbal assaults chiefly target individuals. But sometimes people cause pain by posting false information that everyone can see. For example, Helen Lawson, a nurse in Melbourne, Australia, read about an alternative cancer treatment called black salve. This product is made from a plant called bloodroot, which contains a toxic chemical that can destroy living tissue. Lawson decided to use the black salve to treat her ovarian cancer. The treatment did not work. Lawson died of ovarian cancer. Nevertheless, various Facebook pages—Black Salve Alliance, Bloodroot Black Salves, and Cancer Cures—continue to promote black salve as an effective cancer treatment.

Black salve is just one of many fake remedies promoted on social media. False health claims are also made about vitamins, extracts from the cannabis plant, and many other products. Such false posts can lead sick people away from real medical solutions, prolonging their illness or even causing death.

Much of the medical disinformation is designed to erode confidence in the medical establishment, making consumers more dependent on alternative medical products. During the COVID-19 pandemic, people used social media to spread false claims about the vaccines that were developed to fight the disease. Some of the more outlandish claims suggested that the vaccines would change a person's genetic makeup, turning them into something "not human." Others suggested that the vaccine contained electronic chips that could be tracked by computers. One such meme showed a picture of Microsoft founder Bill Gates with the words "It's simple, we manipulate your DNA with a vaccine, implant you with a [computer] chip, make society cashless and put all money on the chip. Then you will do exactly as you're told or we turn off your chip and you starve until you decide you're ready to be obedient again."[4] The claim, of course, was false.

The Scourge of Disinformation

Social media makes spreading disinformation so easy that the world is awash in it. Disinformation is aimed at the government, businesses, schools, churches, and other pillars of society. While one false post can be dismissed as ridiculous, the accumulation of disinformation can take its toll on social media users, encouraging them to question their trust in traditional institutions. According to a 2020 survey by the Pew Research Center, 64 percent of US adults believe social media is having a negative effect on the way things are going in the United States. Only 10 percent say social media is having a positive effect. The problem mentioned most often was disinformation.

The spread of disinformation is a growing problem, considering the vast number of people who use social media. According to the Pew Research Center, 72 percent of US adults use some type of social media. Among teens, the percentage is even higher. A March 2022 study by Common Sense Media found that 84 percent of US teens use social media. More than three-quarters of US teens and adults are exposed to false and even dangerous speech on a regular basis through social media.

Putting the Vulnerable at Risk

Researchers have found that some of the most harmful words and pictures on social media are not intended to hurt anyone. In fact, the vast majority of those who see this material are not harmed by it. But when people who feel bad about themselves view such posts, the material can make them feel worse. When researchers at Facebook, which owns the photo-sharing app Instagram, asked female teen users if any negative feelings they had in the past month started on Instagram, nearly a third said yes.

Under pressure from watchdog groups, lawmakers, and their own internal research, social media companies have begun to combat disinformation. Facebook, Instagram, Twitter, and YouTube all use a combination of human beings and artificial intelligence to flag and even remove false or misleading information. In 2020 Facebook chief executive officer (CEO) Mark Zuckerberg told Congress that his company placed warnings on more than 150 million posts that independent fact-checkers found to be misleading. Similarly, then-Twitter CEO Jack Dorsey stated that during the 2020 presidential election his company's fact-checking software flagged about three hundred thousand misleading tweets. Both companies also suspended the accounts of people and organizations that repeatedly posted misinformation.

Nevertheless, critics believe more needs to be done. They insist the proliferation of false and deceptive information poses an existential threat to human civilization. As one university professor told the Pew Research Center:

> The internet is the 21st century's threat of a "nuclear winter," and there's no equivalent international framework for nonproliferation or disarmament. The public can grasp the destructive power of nuclear weapons in a way they will never understand the utterly corrosive power of the internet to civilized society, when there is no reliable mechanism for sorting out what people can believe to be true or false.[5]

Chapter One

Is Social Media Use Harmful to Youth Mental Health?

Social Media Use Harms Mental Health in Young People

- Social media creates unrealistic expectations.
- Social media causes negative comparisons.
- Social media promotes personal isolation.

The Debate at a Glance

Social Media Use Benefits Mental Health in Young People

- Studies showing that social media harms mental health are flawed.
- Social media use decreases personal isolation.
- Social media inspires positive changes.

Social Media Use Harms Mental Health in Young People

"It's the ones who are most vulnerable or are already developing a problem—the use of Instagram and other social media can escalate it."

—Angela Guarda, associate professor of psychiatry in the Johns Hopkins University School of Medicine

Quoted in Georgia Wells, Jeff Horvitz, and Deep Seetharaman, "Facebook Knows Instagram Is Toxic for Teen Girls, Company Documents Show," *Wall Street Journal*, September 14, 2021. www.wsj.com.

Consider these questions as you read:

1. How persuasive is the argument that social media presents a distorted view of real life? Explain your answer.
2. Do you think algorithms like Instagram's Explore provide a valuable service? Why or why not?
3. Does using social media change how you feel? If so, in what ways? If not, why not?

Editor's note: The discussion that follows presents common arguments made in support of this perspective, reinforced by facts, quotes, and examples taken from various sources.

A young woman named Michelle suffers from a form of self-doubt known as imposter syndrome. She often feels that she is going to be found out to be a fraud, undeserving of the respect she receives from others. One day, Michelle noticed that her symptoms were worse when she was using social media. "Whether it's another pretty vacation or someone's bouquet of flowers, my mind went from 'Why not me?' to 'I don't deserve those things, and I don't know why,' and it made me feel awful."[6]

From Bad to Worse

Michelle's situation is far from unique. According to 2019 study conducted by Facebook, 21 percent of female and 14 percent

Instagram Worsens Self-Image of Teen Girls

Among teens who reported feeling bad about themselves, one in five said using Instagram made them feel worse. This was the finding of a survey of teen Instagram users conducted by researchers inside Facebook (now Meta), which owns Instagram. The negative impact is greater for girls than for boys, with 21 percent of US girls and 25 percent of UK girls saying that Instagram makes them feel somewhat worse or much worse about themselves.

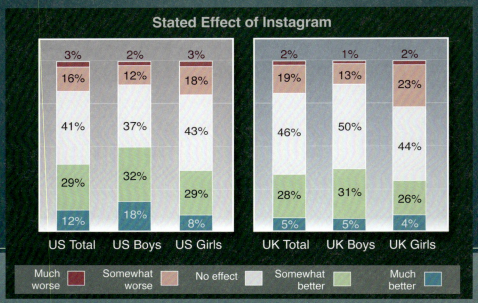

of male teen users say that Instagram makes them feel worse about themselves. The situation is even more serious among those who, like Michelle, are struggling with their mental health. Thirty-one percent of teens with mental health issues say that using Instagram makes them feel worse about themselves.

One problem with social media is that users make comparisons between their own lives and what they see online, and these comparisons often leave them feeling bad. That is because family, friends, and acquaintances only post things that make them look good—like photos of happy moments, exciting places, and wonderful food. Social media users understand that they are only seeing the best moments of other people's lives because they post the same kinds of things, but the effect of seeing everyone else having a great time can bring up feelings of inadequacy or of being left out. "I get really upset when I see other people having the 'perfect' life," says Adnan, a twenty-five-year-old Instagram user. "I am also guilty of trying to show the best side of my life to people."[7]

Users of all social media platforms report having negative feelings, but some apps are worse than others. In 2017 the Royal Society for Public Health (RSPH) in the United Kingdom surveyed almost fifteen hundred young people aged fourteen to twenty-four about their social media experiences. The researchers asked the teens and young adults to rate the impact of different social media platforms on fourteen mental health areas, including anxiety, depression, loneliness, and body image. According to these ratings, YouTube was the most positive platform, followed by Twitter and Facebook. Snapchat and Instagram were rated as most negative. "It's interesting to see Instagram and Snapchat ranking as the worst for mental health and wellbeing," says Shirley Cramer, the chief executive of RSPH. "Both platforms are very image-focused and it appears they may be driving feelings of inadequacy and anxiety in young people."[8] A 2020 study by Facebook, leaked to the public by former Facebook employee Frances Haugen, arrived at the same conclusion. "Teens blame Instagram for increases in the rate of anxiety and depression,"[9] states the report.

> "It's interesting to see Instagram and Snapchat ranking as the worst for mental health and wellbeing. Both platforms are very image-focused and it appears they may be driving feelings of inadequacy and anxiety in young people."[8]
>
> —Shirley Cramer, chief executive of the Royal Society for Public Health

Distorted Reality

One of the problems with Instagram lies within its programming. A software feature known as Explore serves up images that are similar to ones the user has "liked" in the past. These images are not from friends but are posted by people the user does not know or follow. Many of them are posted by professional models and Instagram influencers who take great care to present ideal images of themselves. They wear trendy clothes, use professional lighting, and have perfect hair and makeup. The photos may look like casual selfies, but they are not. They are professional through and through. When users are exposed to a steady stream of idealized images by Explore, they can begin to feel that they do not measure up. "On the face of it, Instagram can look very friendly," says Niamh McDade, a communications executive with RSPH. "But that endless scrolling without much interaction doesn't really lead to much of a positive impact on mental health and wellbeing. You also don't really have control over what you're seeing. And you quite often see images that claim to be showing you reality, yet aren't. That's especially damaging to young men and women."[10]

Instagram's endless parade of healthy, toned bodies can take its toll on users who are struggling with body image issues. This is especially true for teens, who often feel insecure about how they look. Facebook researchers found that among teen girls with Instagram accounts, 32 percent say that when they feel bad about their bodies, Instagram makes them feel worse. One teen girl in the study told the researchers that after scrolling through Instagram, "I feel like I am too big and not pretty enough. It makes me feel insecure about my body even though I know I am skinny."[11] These feelings of inadequacy about their appearance can drive some social media users into unhealthy practices, including purging food that has been consumed or drastically reducing food intake. Angela Guarda, an associate professor of eating disorders at the Johns Hopkins University School of Medicine, says that at least half of her eating disorder patients are influenced by what they see on social media.

A Pathway to Self-Harm

Eating disorders are serious and can even be fatal, but they are not the only dangerous mental health conditions linked to social media use. Facebook researchers found that among teens who reported a desire to engage in self-harm, including cutting, 9 percent said the feelings originated while they were using Instagram. Among those who reported wanting to take their own lives, 6 percent said their suicidal thoughts started on Instagram. Haugen, who leaked the internal documents, is appalled by the findings. "Teenagers are killing themselves because of Instagram,"[12] she says.

> "Teenagers are killing themselves because of Instagram."[12]
>
> —Frances Haugen, former Facebook employee

A British teen named Abby says that Instagram's Explore led her down a rabbit hole into a dark world of self-harm groups, and eventually she tried to take her own life. She says it all began when she liked some sad quotes, and Explore began feeding her more. The algorithm also served up self-harm content, and people unknown to Abby added her to groups in which members encouraged each other to self-harm. "I probably wouldn't have known what self-harm was if I didn't look at those accounts," she says. "You get added into a group, and people would tell me to go kill myself and they'd want to do it together," Abby recalls. The content also included advice on how Abby could take her own life. "I knew how long I would have to stay underwater to drown myself, I knew how many paracetamol I would have to take to kill myself," she says. Abby attempted to take her life, but she survived. She believes her suicide attempt was the result of what she saw on Instagram: "I started really wanting to hurt myself, and I would. . . . But I think apart from that, before then I didn't really want to, and I was just doing it because on Instagram it's glamourised, and it's meant to be like people make it look good."[13]

In December 2021 US surgeon general Vivek Murthy issued an advisory that drew attention to the declining state of youth mental health. "Mental health challenges in children, adolescents, and young adults are real, and they are widespread," stated the surgeon general. Murthy discussed how the media is contributing to the crisis. "We also know that, too often, young people are bombarded with messages through the media and popular culture that erode their sense of self-worth—telling them they are not good looking enough, popular enough, smart enough, or rich enough."[14]

It is time to halt the bombardment of harmful images and messages. According to EarthWeb, a website that analyzes social media, 72 percent of US teens use Instagram every month. The photo-sharing app is the perfect place to begin making social media a safer place for American youth.

Social Media Use Benefits Mental Health in Young People

"Screen use was incredibly important to young people. . . . It was really important for them to stay connected to other friends; to keep their mood up, be entertained and pass the time, get inspiration and express their creativity, and protect their mental health in terms of connecting with young people."

—Victoria Rideout, independent researcher on children and the media

Quoted in Ilana Lowery, "Using Common Sense: Media Use by Tweens and Teens on the Rise," Raising Arizona Kids, April 26, 2022. www.raisingarizonakids.com.

Consider these questions as you read:

1. Do you agree with the perspective that the media reports negative views about social media without asking deeper questions? Explain your answer.
2. Do you or someone you know feel worse after using social media? What about feeling better? Describe some examples of the feelings you have had or heard about that reflect social media use.
3. How persuasive is that argument that most young people feel better after using social media? Explain your answer.

Editor's note: The discussion that follows presents common arguments made in support of this perspective, reinforced by facts, quotes, and examples taken from various sources.

When Frances Haugen leaked internal Facebook research to the public, dozens of media outlets uncritically repeated her allegations that Instagram, which Facebook owns, is harmful to teens. "Facebook Documents Show How Toxic Instagram Is for Teens," stated CNBC. "Facebook Is a Harmful Presence in Our Lives," declared the *Guardian*. "Facebook Knows Instagram Contributes to Eating Disorders," reported Business Insider. However, a careful analysis of the research paints an entirely different picture than the one in the headlines. Instagram is not nearly as harmful as Haugen and the media make it out to be. In fact, the app is a mostly positive influence on teen users, including those with mental health problems.

Misleading Numbers

The Facebook research statistics quoted in the media are misleading. One of the most troubling findings was that 6 percent of US teens and 13 percent of UK teens who reported having thoughts about suicide said that the idea originated on Instagram. But the media reports never say how many teens had thought about suicide in the first place. If every teen had such thoughts, then the percentages would be frighteningly high. But that was not the case. The Facebook study found that 82 individuals, 3 percent of the 2,543 teens surveyed, had thought about suicide in the past month. In that smaller group, or subset, five US teens and eleven UK teens said that their suicidal thoughts started on Instagram. Those sixteen individuals make up less than 1 percent of all the teens surveyed. "Of course, even one person who feels this started on Instagram is one too many," states the report. "That is why we have invested so heavily in support, resources and interventions for people using our services."[15] Still, the media never mentions that more than 99 percent of the teens in the survey did not have suicidal thoughts traceable to Instagram.

The issue of subsets applies to the explosive headlines about Instagram making teen girls feel worse about body image. The survey did not find that one out of three female users said that Instagram made them feel worse about their bodies. Instead, it found that one out three female users who already felt bad about their bodies said that Instagram made them feel worse. The number who said they already felt bad was about 450 teens, or about 18 percent of those surveyed. Of those, 150 said Instagram made them feel worse—one-third of the subset but only 6 percent of the overall sample. "The finding does not describe a

Using Instagram Makes Teens Feel Better

Teen Instagram users say they are not negatively affected by their use of that social media platform. In fact, many contend it actually makes them feel better in all sorts of ways. This was the finding of a 2021 survey of 2,543 US and UK teens by Facebook (now Meta), which owns Instagram. Among teens who reported experiencing a mental health issue in the month prior to the survey, a large number said that viewing Instagram made them feel better about themselves or had no impact. The percentage of teens who felt worse because of their interactions with Instagram was, in nearly all instances, small.

Question: What impact did Instagram have on this experience?

Category	Made it worse	No impact	Made it better
Problematic social media use	31.1%	37.2%	31.7%
Social comparison	22.7%	42.4%	34.9%
Body image	18.9%	56.4%	24.7%
Fear of missing out	18.6%	40.7%	40.7%
Sleep issues	17.7%	53.2%	29.1%
Suicide Ideation	15.3%	45.5%	39.2%
Anxiety	14.8%	44.3%	40.9%
Loneliness	14.7%	39.9%	45.4%
Eating issues	12.9%	61.1%	26%
Sadness	10.8%	40.3%	48.9%
Financial stress	7.7%	62.6%	29.7%
Family stress	7.1%	49.6%	43.3%
Work stress	6.5%	52%	41.5%

Source: Meta, "Instagram Is More Likely to Make Things Better than Worse," September 26, 2021. https://about.fb.com.

random sampling of teenage girls, or even all the girls in the survey," says Anya Kamenetz, a correspondent for NPR who analyzed the report. "It's a subset of a subset of a subset."[16]

Feeling Better Rather than Worse

After the internal research was leaked to the press, Facebook released the full report. It shows that even among teen girls who felt bad about their bodies, the vast majority—67 percent—said that Instagram did not make them feel worse. In fact, 22 percent said that Instagram made them feel better about their body image. The remaining 45 percent said it did not affect them either way.

In eleven out of the twelve categories of mental health issues the survey asked about, more teen girls said that Instagram made them feel better than said it made them feel worse. For example, when it came to eating issues, 24 percent of teen girls said Instagram made them feel better, while 17 percent said it made them feel worse. The majority—59 percent—said it had no effect at all. The contrast is even more significant when it comes to social comparison. Forty-two percent of teen girls said Instagram made them feel better about social comparisons. Only 20 percent said it made them feel worse. Thirty-eight percent said it had no effect.

And so it was, all down the list of issues—anxiety, fear of missing out, sleep issues, social support, loneliness, sadness, financial stress, and family stress. For sadness, 57 percent of teen girls who had experienced a mental health issue in the previous thirty days said Instagram made them feel better, while only 9 percent said it made them feel worse. Among boys who had experienced a mental health issue in the previous thirty days, the number who said Instagram made them feel better was larger (often much larger) than the number who said it made them feel worse in all twelve categories. For all teens in the survey who had experienced a mental health issue in the previous thirty days, the positive effects of Instagram outnumbered the negative effects in every mental health category.

Unreliable Data

Another problem with the Facebook research is that it relied on the self-reporting of the teens in the survey without confirming the results using any other method. According to Candice Odgers, a psychologist who has conducted scientific studies of the effects of social media on teens, just asking teens how they feel is not enough. That is because many teens have heard that social media can be bad for them, and their survey answers are often shaped by that knowledge. "If you ask teens if they are addicted/harmed by social media or their phones, the vast majority say yes," says Odgers. "But if you actually do the research and connect their use to objective measures . . . there is very little to no connection."[17]

> "If you ask teens if they are addicted/harmed by social media or their phones, the vast majority say yes. But if you actually do the research . . . there is very little to no connection."[17]
>
> —Candice Odgers, psychologist

The Positive Effects of Social Media

Other researchers have used proven scientific techniques to look at the same kinds of issues that the Facebook researchers did, and the results of these studies suggest that the Facebook research did not exaggerate the positive effects of social media. In fact, a 2021 study for Common Sense Media found that social media has even more positive effects on mental health than Facebook found.

The Common Sense Media researchers surveyed a scientifically selected, nationally representative group of fifteen hundred US youths aged fourteen to twenty years. The researchers used the widely recognized PHQ-8 scale to measure symptoms of depression. They found that 43 percent of respondents said that when they feel depressed, stressed, or anxious, using social media usually makes them feel better. This compared to just 17 percent who said it makes them feel worse. (The others said it makes

> "Young people are far more likely to say that using social media makes them feel better rather than worse when they are feeling down."[18]
>
> —Common Sense Media study

no difference either way.) The number saying social media had a positive effect represented a dramatic 59 percent increase from 2018, when just 27 percent said social media made them feel better. "Young people are far more likely to say that using social media makes them feel better rather than worse when they are feeling down,"[18] stated the researchers.

The Common Sense Media study turned up an important finding regarding social media users who have moderate to severe depressive symptoms. The researchers found that 29 percent of users with depressive symptoms say social media is very important for getting inspiration from others. Just 17 percent of those without symptoms say the same thing. Similarly, 28 percent of those with depressive symptoms say that social media is very important for feeling less alone, while only 13 percent of those without depressive symptoms say that. Significantly for suicide prevention, 26 percent of those with depressive symptoms say social media is very important for getting support or advice when needed—a figure that has more than doubled since 2018. Only 15 percent of those without such symptoms believe the same thing. This research suggests that parents and leaders who limit access to social media by teens with depressive symptoms because of the Facebook research might be doing exactly the wrong thing. They are cutting a lifeline to those who need it most.

Chapter Two

Should Social Media Companies Regulate Speech?

Social Media Companies Should Regulate Speech

- Social media is filled with harmful and dangerous content that spreads exponentially.
- Social media companies need to take responsibility for content that appears on their platforms.
- More aggressive monitoring and removal of misinformation and hate speech is the least companies can do to protect users and the public.
- Social media companies should ban people who spread misinformation and hate speech.

The Debate at a Glance

Social Media Companies Should Not Regulate Free Speech

- Social media companies should not be the arbiters of what constitutes appropriate and inappropriate speech.
- Users should be allowed to see all points of view.
- Social media users can decide for themselves what is true and what is false.
- Censorship causes more problems than it solves.

Social Media Companies Should Regulate Speech

"The goal of these [disinformation] tools is not necessarily to create consistent and believable alternative facts, but to create plausible levels of doubt in actual facts. The crisis we face about truth and reliable facts is predicated less on the ability to get people to believe the wrong thing as it is on the ability to get people to doubt the right thing."

—Jamais Cascio, Distinguished Fellow at the Institute for the Future

Quoted in Science, Technology & the Future, *Jamais Cascio—Are 'Alternative Facts' Created to Be Believed, or to Cast Doubt on Reality?*, YouTube, November 27, 2020. https://youtu.be/F8gRfw2d_ls.

Consider these questions as you read:

1. What should people do when they come across false statements or disinformation on social media?
2. Do you agree with the argument that disinformation is eroding confidence in various institutions? Explain your answer.
3. Do you think social media companies should be doing more to identify and remove disinformation? Why or why not?

Editor's note: The discussion that follows presents common arguments made in support of this perspective, reinforced by facts, quotes, and examples taken from various sources.

In April 2020, not long after the COVID-19 pandemic had broken out, millions of people, unsure of how the virus was spread, were rubbing disinfectant on their hands, grocery cart handles, and even packages of food they bought at the store to protect themselves from the deadly virus. On April 5, in the midst of the fears about the pandemic, a thirty-nine-year-old man named Christopher Charles Perez posted a disturbing message on Facebook about an H-E-B grocery store in San Antonio, Texas: "My homeboys cousin has covid19 and has licked everything for past two days cause we paid him too. YOU'VE BEEN WARNED." Shortly afterward, Perez posted another message on Facebook. It linked to a news story about a different store that had been forced to close after an employee had tested positive for COVID-19. "Lol, I did try to warn y'all," wrote Perez. "Nogalitos location next,"[19] he added, referring to an H-E-B supermarket located on Nogalitos Street in San Antonio.

Using Social Media to Spread Terror

Perez's first post was untrue. No one licked any groceries. Perez removed the post after sixteen minutes. The threat in the second post was also false, although the news story about the store closing was true. Perez took down the second post after about twenty-three hours. However, an anonymous person took a screenshot of the first post and forwarded it to law enforcement officials who investigate criminal and terrorist activity. Perez was charged with spreading false information and hoaxes related to biological weapons. In June 2021 a jury found Perez guilty, and a federal judge sentenced him to fifteen months in federal prison. "Perez's actions were knowingly designed to spread fear and panic," Christopher Combs, the head the Federal Bureau of Investigation's San Antonio field office, said in the statement. The sentence, Combs added, "illustrates the seriousness of this crime."[20]

Perez's case reveals one of the greatest flaws of social media—namely, that anyone can post anything at any time. Postings can be true; they can be false; they can be informative; they can be misleading. Unlike traditional media, there is no editor to review posts before they are released to the public. And while social media companies have developed automatic filters to flag potentially dangerous information, these filters are slow and imperfect. A threatening post can be seen be thousands, even millions, before questions are raised, if they are raised at all.

An Explosion of Unreliable Information

Although credible sources still predominate on social media, the amount of unreliable information being shared is rapidly multiplying. This calls for strong action by social media companies to fight misinformation and disinformation on their platforms. According to an analysis using NewsGuard, a journalism and technology tool that rates the credibility of news and information, in 2019 there were 8.6 billion engagements with news sources on social media. Of these, 0.7 billion, or 8 percent, came from sources deemed unreliable. In contrast, of the 16.3 billion engagements with news sources on social media in 2020, the analysis identified 2.8 billion, or 17 percent, as unreliable sources.

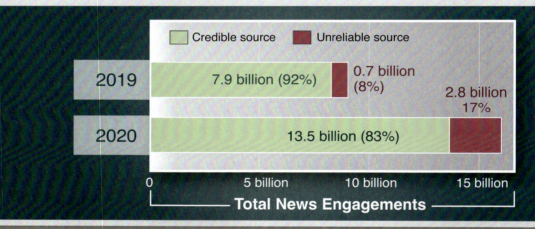

Source: Sara Fischer, "'Unreliable' News Sources Got More Traction in 2020," Axios, December 22, 2020. www.axios.com.

The High Cost of Disinformation

Admittedly, the majority of social media posts are harmless. But for the few with the desire and know-how to sow disinformation, social media offers untold opportunities to create mischief. For example, in 2017 would-be investors in the cryptocurrency known as ETH spread the rumor that Vitalik Buterin, the founder of the company behind ETH, had died in a car crash. Fearing that the company would falter without Buterin's leadership and the value of ETH would decline, investors began to sell ETH to get as much profit as they could out of it before it collapsed.

The sell-off caused the value of the digital tokens to plunge $4 billion within hours. When the price was low, the people behind the hoax bought as much as ETH as they could. Once investors learned that Buterin was still alive, the value of ETH rebounded. The hoaxers made a fortune as the value of their tokens skyrocketed. Those who sold ETH lost billions.

Money is the motivation behind many online scams, but financial greed is only part of the problem. Disinformation is often used to advance causes that supporters believe are so important that the noble ends justify the dishonest means. Political parties spread false information to influence voters and gain power. Radical environmentalists defame corporations to hurt their sales and slow their consumption of natural resources. Anarchists and revolutionaries sow distrust in governments to weaken their control over society and pave the way for social change. The result is a sea of disinformation that is seeping into the feeds of billions of social media users, who often believe that what they are reading is true. These lies are undermining democracy itself. "On page one of any political science textbook it will say that democracy relies on people being informed about the issues so they can have a debate and make a decision," says Stephan Lewandowsky, a cognitive scientist at the University of Bristol in the United Kingdom. "Having a large number of people in a society who are misinformed and have their own set of facts is absolutely devastating and extremely difficult to cope with."[21]

> "Having a large number of people in a society who are misinformed and have their own set of facts is absolutely devastating and extremely difficult to cope with."[21]
>
> —Stephan Lewandowsky, cognitive scientist at the University of Bristol

The Need for Self-Policing

There is only one way to stem the rising tide of disinformation: social media companies need to take control of what is being posted. Twitter, Facebook, YouTube, and Instagram have already taken steps to flag or remove disinformation, but they need to do more. Right now, the social media giants use artificial intelligence aided by human beings to identify posts containing false or misleading information. Facebook covers problematic posts with a gray screen bearing the words: "False Information. The same information was checked in another post by independent fact-checkers." The user can click on the screen to remove it and see the post or click on an icon to see why the post was flagged. Twitter identifies false or misleading tweets with a light blue exclamation point and a statement explaining why the tweet has been flagged.

In August 2021 Facebook reported that it removed 20 million pieces of COVID-19 misinformation from the platform. The company also banned 3,000 accounts, pages, and groups that were spreading COVID-19-related misinformation. This is encouraging, but considering that users post 657 million tweets and 422 million Facebook status updates every day, the number of flagged and removed posts is infinitesimal.

Facebook says it is serious about combating disinformation. "We've invested heavily in people and technology to keep our platform safe, and have made fighting misinformation and providing authoritative information a priority,"[22] says Lena Pietsch, Facebook's director of policy communications. The company says it has forty thousand people working on safety and security and has spent $13 billion in those areas over the past six years. That may be true, but "safety and security" covers many things other than disinformation, including guarding against hackers and responding to user complaints about harassment and bullying.

Underfunded and Understaffed

Frances Haugen, a former Facebook employee who worked in the company's civic integrity unit, questions how much the company is doing to combat misinformation. She stated in an interview, "We have no independent transparency mechanisms that allow us to see what Facebook is doing internally." Haugen added that her department, which monitors posts that violate the organization's community standards, was understaffed when she worked at Facebook. "Our team at any given time only could work on a third of the cases that we had," she revealed. "We could've had, you know, two, three, ten times as many people."[23]

> "Our [information monitoring] team at any given time only could work on a third of the cases that we had. We could've had, you know, two, three, ten times as many people."[23]
>
> —Frances Haugen, former Facebook employee

The consumer data company Statista estimates that social media companies generated advertising revenues exceeding $50 billion in 2021 alone. The social media giants have the money they need to do a better job of monitoring, flagging, and removing disinformation. They need to invest in more and better artificial intelligence to remove not just some disinformation but nearly all of it before it has a chance to spread its poison through society.

Social Media Companies Should Not Regulate Free Speech

"Free speech is the bedrock of a functioning democracy, and Twitter is the digital town square where matters vital to the future of humanity are debated."

—Elon Musk, business magnate and investor

Quoted in Twitter, "Elon Musk to Acquire Twitter," Cision PR Newswire, April 25, 2022. www.prnewswire.com.

Consider these questions as you read:

1. Do you agree with the idea that the truth will prevail over falsehood in free and open debate? Explain your answer and support it with an example.
2. Do you think that false information needs to be protected from censorship, especially on the internet? Explain your answer.
3. Do you think that flagging some social media posts as false will discourage other people from expressing their opinions? Why or why not?

Editor's note: The discussion that follows presents common arguments made in support of this perspective, reinforced by facts, quotes, and examples taken from various sources.

On October 14, 2020, just twenty days before the 2020 presidential election, the *New York Post* published an exposé regarding the business dealings of Hunter Biden, the son of then–presidential candidate Joe Biden. The story was based on emails that were recovered from Hunter Biden's MacBook Pro laptop that the owner of a Delaware computer shop said had been dropped off for repair in April 2019 and never picked up. The emails allegedly contradicted claims that Joe Biden had no connection to foreign influences from China, Ukraine, and other nations while serving as vice president under Barack Obama. The article appeared online at 5:00 a.m. At 8:10 a.m. Facebook spokesperson Andy

Stone announced that the social media giant was limiting access to the Hunter Biden news story on its platform while its fact checkers worked to verify the accuracy of the story. By 2:20 p.m. Twitter, which also expressed concerns about the authenticity of the story, had barred users from sharing links to the news story. Twitter also locked the account of the *New York Post*, preventing it from publishing any more information. It was the first time a social media platform had suspended the account of a news organization.

In their zeal to prevent disinformation from affecting the upcoming election, Twitter and Facebook committed the most consequential act of news suppression in recent history. A survey taken after the election by pollster John McLaughlin found that 4.6 percent of Biden voters said they would have switched their votes if they had known about the *New York Post* stories about Hunter Biden. Amid fears that foreign governments might interfere with the 2020 presidential election, it was instead the social media companies that ran interference.

An Error in Judgment

Most importantly, the concerns of the social media companies were completely unfounded. On March 30, 2022, the *Washington Post* reported that it had hired two computer experts to evaluate twenty-two thousand emails from the Hunter Biden laptop. The experts found that the emails were authentic. Both Facebook and Twitter had suppressed a story that was 100 percent true.

The silencing of the *New York Post* reveals exactly why social media companies should not be in the business of regulating speech: no one entity can decide what is true and what is not true, especially in the short term. For example, in the field of science, a researcher who proves a hypothesis in a laboratory must have the results confirmed by other scientists before it is accepted as true. Even then, many scientific findings believed to be true have later been shown to be only partially true or even false. If the truth is difficult to establish in the field of science, which follows exacting standards and processes, it is even more difficult for

Americans Do Not Trust Social Media Companies to Censor Data

More than two-thirds of US adults (67 percent) have little or no confidence in the ability of social media companies to decide which posts to label as inaccurate or misleading. This was the finding of a June 2020 survey by the Pew Research Center. The distrust was higher among Republicans (84 percent) than among Democrats (52 percent). However, large numbers on both sides of the political divide do not trust the social media companies to decide what is true and what is false.

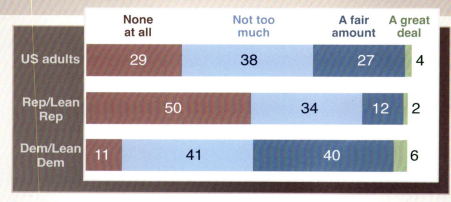

% of US adults who say they have _____ (of) confidence in social media companies to determine which posts on their platforms should be labeled as inaccurate or misleading

	None at all	Not too much	A fair amount	A great deal
US adults	29	38	27	4
Rep/Lean Rep	50	34	12	2
Dem/Lean Dem	11	41	40	6

Note: Strongly/somewhat approve or disapprove responses are combined. Those who did not give an answer are not shown.

Source: Emily A. Vogels, Andrew Perrin, and Monica Anderson, "Most Americans Think Social Media Sites Censor Political Viewpoints," Pew Research Center, August 19, 2020. www.pewresearch.org.

social media companies to do so when evaluating the accuracy of news reporting. The *New York Post* followed its own journalistic standards before publishing the Hunter Biden laptop story. The reporter had multiple sources, and the story was carefully reviewed by editors prior to publication. The paper had every reason to believe its story was true. Nevertheless, the social media companies—without the background and information available to the *New York Post*—took it upon themselves to evaluate the truth of the story, and they concluded it was false. And it bears repeating: they were wrong.

Discovering the Truth Through Debate

The entire process of fact-checking and censorship practiced by the social media giants is antithetical to the process of discovering the truth as it has evolved over hundreds of years. At one time in the Western world, the Catholic Church and various monarchs decided what was true, what was false, and what could be said in public. In 1633 the Catholic Church famously forced the Italian scientist Galileo Galilei to recant his finding that the earth moves around the sun, because even though the theory was correct, it conflicted with church doctrine. In England, Parliament passed the Ordinance for the Regulating of Printing in 1643, requiring authors to have their work approved by the government before it could be published. Books and pamphlets deemed false or dangerous were not allowed to be published, a practice known as prior restraint. In a 1644 speech entitled *Areopagitica*, English poet and scholar John Milton criticized the practice of prior restraint, arguing that it was better to allow the public to see all competing ideas and determine what is true through debate: "And though all the winds of doctrine were let loose to play upon the earth, so Truth be in the field, we do injuriously, by licensing and prohibiting, to misdoubt her strength. Let her and Falsehood grapple; who ever knew Truth put to the worse, in a free and open encounter?"[24]

The idea that the public can decide for itself what is true and what is false is the bedrock principle underlying the practice of free speech. This principle was enshrined in law in England and then in the United States, and it has been adopted in many other countries as well. It rejects the idea that any person or group of persons can or should determine what is true and what is false prior to publication. The protection against prior restraint is enshrined in the First Amendment to the US Constitution, which states, "Congress shall make no law . . . abridging the freedom of speech, or of the press."

> "Let [Truth] and Falsehood grapple; who ever knew Truth put to the worse, in a free and open encounter?"[24]
>
> —John Milton, poet and scholar

Protecting All Speech

The guarantee of free speech applies to all expression because the framers of the Constitution believed that no experts, no fact-checkers, and no authorities are qualified to determine the truth of an idea. Only the public can sort it out. As a result, the First Amendment protects both true statements and false ones. "Erroneous statement is inevitable in free debate," wrote Supreme Court justice William Brennan in a free speech case known as *New York Times Co. v. Sullivan* (1964), "and . . . it must be protected if the freedoms of expression are to have the 'breathing space' that they 'need . . . to survive.'"[25]

> "Erroneous statement is inevitable in free debate, and . . . it must be protected if the freedoms of expression are to have the 'breathing space' that they 'need . . . to survive."[25]
>
> —William Brennan, justice of the Supreme Court

It is worth remembering that some ideas now widely accepted as true were once believed to be false. For example, the idea that women should be able to vote and run for office was extremely unpopular at one time. It was only through decades of debate protected by the First Amendment that popular opinion changed and Congress passed and the states ratified the Nineteenth Amendment, guaranteeing women the right to vote. Many other ideas and causes, including the civil rights movement, also gained acceptance through free and open debate.

The Return of the Censors

Because Facebook, Twitter, Instagram, YouTube, and other social media platforms are private companies, the First Amendment does not apply directly to them. They are allowed to practice prior restraint and block posts they believe to be false or misleading. However, in doing so, they are adopting a model of governing speech that is contrary to the one that has worked so well for hundreds of years. They also are creating new problems. By flagging posts, they are intimidating people from posting their views on social media out of fear of being ridiculed. This is having a chilling effect on free speech and is another form of suppression.

The arrogance of the social media giants is breathtaking. Like the autocrats of old, they believe they can decide what the public should see and what it should not. Being wrong about the Hunter Biden laptop story should have been enough to humble Facebook and Twitter into abandoning their practice of prior restraint, but it was not. Therefore, it is up to political leaders, free speech advocates, and social media users to demand change. It is up to the people to compel social media organizations to comply with the same standards of free speech that democracies embrace.

Chapter Three

Is Social Media Addictive?

Social Media Is Addictive

- Social media software is designed to increase engagement to the point of being addictive.
- Social media addiction has real-world consequences, including disrupted lives and relationships.
- The inability to control social media use—even when it is harmful—is a clear sign of addiction.

The Debate at a Glance

Social Media Is Not Addictive

- Social media overuse is a bad habit, not an addiction.
- What some people call an addiction is instead a symptom of an underlying mental health condition, such as depression.
- Overuse of social media is often a sign of a real addiction, such as drug abuse or alcoholism.

Social Media Is Addictive

"It really is an addiction, and we're wired for this. The same brain pathways get stimulated as they do in a chemical addiction."

—Joshua Ehrlich, psychologist

Quoted in Rebecca Fishbein, "How to Kick a Mindless Scrolling Habit," Forge, August 12, 2019. https://forge.medium.com.

Consider these questions as you read:

1. Do you think the comparison between social media use and gambling behaviors is accurate? Explain your answer.
2. Do you think a behavioral addiction is comparable to a chemical addiction? Why or why not?
3. Have you ever experienced the fear of missing out because you did not have access to social media? How did you feel?

Editor's note: The discussion that follows presents common arguments made in support of this perspective, reinforced by facts, quotes, and examples taken from various sources.

In a post entitled "Heavily addicted to scrolling and refreshing social media/YouTube/the forum . . . etc.," social media user Javfly33 says he has become dependent on the small doses of dopamine—a feel-good chemical produced in the brain—that he receives when scrolling through social media posts. "Since a while I've been heavily addicted to what I described in the title," he wrote in a 2021 post on Actualized.org, an online self-improvement forum.

> I don't exactly [know] why but it's insane. I refresh and scroll HUNDREDS of times during the day Instagram, WhatsApp mainly. . . . I refresh over and over and most of the times I don't even read the messages of the people here. It's like my brain is broken for dopamine Lol. . . .

It's gotten bad to the point that sometimes I can't read a large text or something like that because it seems I need to go to the next thing.

And the next, and the next, and the next.[26]

Javfly33 makes light of the dopamine "high" he experiences when using social media, but it is not a laughing matter. It is real, and it is the main cause of social media addiction.

Manipulating the Brain

Discovered in 1957, dopamine is one of about twenty major neurotransmitters, chemicals that carry signals between neurons, nerves, and other cells in the body. Dopamine is part of a natural reward system. It creates a sense of well-being when a person learns or achieves something. Typically, dopamine rewards a behavior that is vital to life, such as drinking when thirsty or eating when hungry. Such rewards create and reinforce life-sustaining habits. "We found a signal in the brain that explains our most profound behaviours, in which every one of us is engaged constantly,"[27] says Wolfram Schultz, a professor of neuroscience at Cambridge University in England, who was the first to recognize the role that dopamine plays in the brain.

Since Shultz's discoveries in the 1980s, scientists have observed that dopamine can be released when people engage in activities that are not essential to survival, including sports and even gambling. "When a gambler feels favoured by luck, dopamine is released,"[28] reports Natasha Schüll, a professor at New York University. The feeling of well-being that engulfs gamblers when they win even small amounts of money helps keep them interested in playing. Typically, the longer they play, the more money they lose. This is why gambling machines, such as slot machines, reward players with many small payouts and the occasional large one. The machines are designed to manipulate the release of dopamine by interspersing a few wins with many more losses.

Social media apps have been engineered to manipulate the brain just as slot machines do. Users receive occasional rewards in the form of likes, comments, and shares that release small amounts of dopamine. "Social reward, in the form of likes and comments, is very reinforcing," says Erin A. Vogel, a social psychologist. "We feel good when we get social reward, so we keep posting."[29] The process of posting content, receiving likes and comments, and refreshing to see whether the post has garnered more positive feedback can be addicting. "In terms of drugs, we know that the faster something reaches your brain, the more addicting it is, since it lights up your brain's reward system so quickly," says Vogel. "Social media engagement is instantaneous; you upload a photo, you get validation, you want more."[30]

> "Social media engagement is instantaneous; you upload a photo, you get validation, you want more."[30]
>
> —Erin A. Vogel, social psychologist

Social media insiders say that the dopamine-triggering features of social media were put in place for the same reason that they are used in slot machines: to keep people engaged with the app for as long as possible. The more time users spend on an app, the more ads they will see—and the more money the social media company will make. "In order to get your stock price up, the amount of time that people spend on your app has to go up," says software designer Aza Raskin. "So, when you put that much pressure on that one number, you're going to start trying to invent new ways of getting people to stay hooked."[31]

A Behavioral Addiction

Although using social media releases the chemical dopamine in the brain, social media addiction is not considered a chemical addiction, like an addiction to alcohol or opioids. Instead, it is a behavioral addiction, akin to gambling disorder or shopping addiction. *Behavioral addiction* describes a situation in which a person repeatedly engages in an activity and is unable to stop doing so, even when the behavior causes harm to the person.

As with chemical addiction, one of the telltale signs of a behavioral addiction is that it creates conflict in an individual's

Rising Number of People Potentially Addicted to Social Media

Researchers at Influencer Marketing Hub estimate that the number of people potentially addicted to social media worldwide has increased almost 60 percent between 2017 and 2022. Using data from a study published in the journal *Technology In Society*, they estimated that that number rose from 210 million in 2017 to 333 million in 2022.

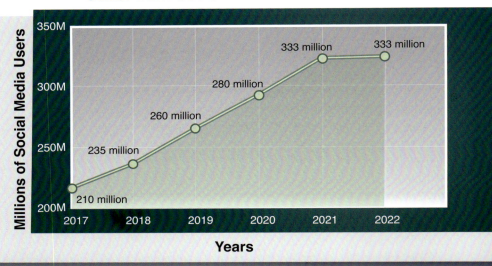

Estimated Number of People Who Potentially Suffer from Social Media Addiction in 2022

Source: Werner Geyser, "The Real Social Media Addiction Stats for 2022," Influencer Marketing Hub, August 3, 2022. https://influencermarketinghub.com.

personal, family, or professional life. Relationships suffer, schoolwork deteriorates, friends drift away. However, a worsening life is not by itself proof that a person has an addiction, according to Mark D. Griffiths, a professor at Nottingham Trent University in England. For example, people might realize that their behavior is having harmful effects on their life and decide to cut back on or even stop using social media. But people who are addicted typically cannot break away on their own. If they do, they suffer withdrawal symptoms—that is, unpleasant feelings or physical sensations when not able to engage in a behavior. Such feelings often cause addicted users to relapse, or revert to excessive use. According to Griffiths, other signs of social media addiction include salience, when a behavior becomes the most important part of a person's life; mood modification, when a person uses a behavior to alter moods or escape from problems; and tolerance, when a person has to spend more time engaged in a behavior to produce the same sense of well-being. When social media use meets these six criteria—conflict, salience, mood modification, tolerance, withdrawal symptoms, and relapse—it is a behavioral addiction.

> "I'm completely consumed by the urge to check all the social media platforms I occupy pretty much every minute of the day and it's destroying my entire existence."[33]
>
> —Chrissa Hardy, senior editor for the online publication Wise Bread

Motivated by Fear

One of the most common reasons for mood modification among social media users is to alleviate a form of anxiety known as fear of missing out, or FOMO. Researchers at the University of Essex in England define FOMO as "the uneasy and sometimes all-consuming feeling that you're missing out—that your peers are doing, in the know about, or in possession of more or something better than you."[32]

Chrissa Hardy, a senior editor for the online publication Wise Bread, says that FOMO has made her a social media addict. "I have a problem," she writes. "I'm completely consumed by the urge to check all the social media platforms I occupy pretty much every minute of the day and it's destroying my entire existence. You probably think I'm exaggerating—we all go on social media all the time, right? Well, I do it way, way too much. . . . It's the FOMO that keeps my mind occupied, and has me coming back again and again."[33]

When people check their social media accounts to alleviate the anxiety of FOMO, they are engaged in modifying their mood—a hallmark of behavioral addiction. They are not acting out of curiosity. They are compelled by the FOMO to engage with their social media app. "You let it go from being something you enjoy to something that's controlling you,"[34] says Douglas Gentile, a professor of psychology at Iowa State University. When people have lost control of their choices and actions, they are addicted.

Social Media Is Not Addictive

"The overwhelming majority of social media users are NOT pathologically addicted."

—Nir Eyal, author and lecturer

Nir Eyal, "Can We Please Stop Calling Everyone 'Addicted'?," *Nir and Far* (podcast), November 28, 2021. www.nirandfar.com.

Consider these questions as you read:

1. Is the fact that the American Psychiatric Association does not recognize social media addiction as a disorder a persuasive argument that it is not an addiction? Explain your answer.
2. Are you persuaded that social media overuse is usually a symptom of an underlying disorder, rather than a sign of addiction? Explain your answer.
3. Have you ever felt addicted to social media? Could you stop using it? Why or why not?

Editor's note: The discussion that follows presents common arguments made in support of this perspective, reinforced by facts, quotes, and examples taken from various sources.

It is an exaggeration to say that people are addicted to social media. Many people overuse social media. Some have made checking their social media accounts a habit. But their behavior lacks key elements of a true addiction. In particular, few if any social media users experience withdrawal symptoms so acute that quitting on their own is impossible. And even fewer relapse into the behavior once they have stopped. To say people are addicted to social media is itself harmful. It suggests that people are powerless to change their behavior when they are not.

Not a Recognized Addiction

The best-known authority on addiction is the American Psychiatric Association (APA). Every few years it publishes a book to guide mental health professionals in properly diagnosing disorders. The most recent version of this book, the fifth edition of the *Diagnostic and Statistical Manual of Mental Disorders* (DSM-5), published in 2013, describes several behavioral addictions, including gambling disorder, eating disorders, and shopping addiction. However, it does not include social media overuse as any kind of disorder, dependency, or addiction. The manual does not include any internet-related overuse as a mental disorder, even though internet addiction was first suggested as a disorder as far back as 1996.

Although the APA has not designated any internet behavior as an addiction, the DSM-5 does include a condition known as internet gaming disorder (IGD), in its appendix. The manual offers proposed diagnostic criteria for the disorder and encourages mental health professionals to use the criteria to see whether IGD should be included as a disorder in the DSM-6.

A Lack of Intensity

Although social media overuse and IGD both involve technology, experts see a big difference in intensity between browsing social media and playing a video game. Video game players often remain highly focused on games for hours on end and can be extremely reluctant to stop playing. Because of their deep involvement with their gaming, they may lie about how much they are playing, allow their job or schoolwork to suffer, and experience withdrawal symptoms when unable to play. While social media users may spend hours scrolling through posts, the intensity of the experience is not as great as in game playing. Rarely do social media users experience withdrawal symptoms when they stop using the apps.

A simple online search of "how I quit social media" will turn up hundreds of stories of people who gave up social media simply by deleting the apps and finding new ways to fill their time—walking, exercising, reading books, or playing a musical instrument. This is not true with some gamers, who end up having to sell or destroy their devices or even seek counseling to end their habits. And neither social media overuse nor video gaming are as addictive as, say, gambling, in which those with a disorder often wager larger and larger sums of money, lose all their financial assets, and even go into debt to continue their habit. That is a true addiction.

Financial Incentive

One of the reasons that some mental health professionals are pushing for the APA to recognize social media overuse as an addiction or disorder is that it would open a new and potentially lucrative practice. Once a disorder is listed in the DSM, medical insurance will help pay for its treatment. Because of the large number of people who overuse social media, an official designation in the DSM would provide a financial windfall for treatment centers and individual counselors.

One downside of recognizing social media overuse as an official disorder is that more authorized treatment would cause medical insurance rates—which are already high—to go even higher as insurers are forced to pay for treatment. In addition, mental health resources needed to treat drug addiction, eating disorders, and other serious mental health conditions would be stretched thin as more and more counselors spent their time treating social media disorder.

Underlying Causes

There is no doubt that some people overuse social media and have a hard time giving it up. But in many of these cases, the person showing signs of social media addiction already has an underlying mental health condition, such as depression, anxiety disorder, mood disorder, behavioral disorders, autism spectrum disorder, attention-deficit/hyperactivity disorder (ADHD), or even substance abuse. For example, a 2021 study by Common Sense Media, a nonprofit organization that studies media and technology, found that young people with depressive symptoms are nearly twice as likely as those without depression to say they use social media almost constantly (34 percent versus 18 percent).

Distribution of Overuse Factors Across Platforms

Social media overuse is nearly always the result of underlying mental health factors. This was the finding of a 2021 study by researchers in the United Kingdom. Their study of Twitter, Instagram, and Facebook found that loneliness, fear of missing out, and low self-control are among the chief factors behind excessive use of all three platforms. Other conditions are more common to particular platforms. Nevertheless, mental health issues are the common factor in overuse.

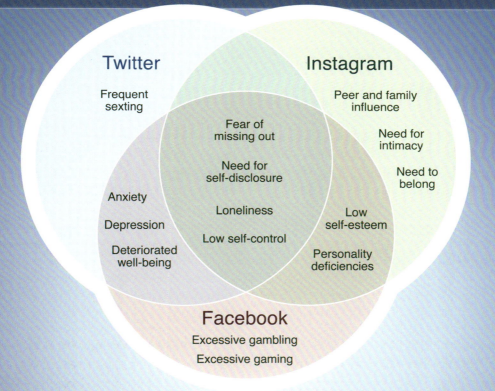

Overuse Factors Across Social Media Platforms

Source: Hosam Al-Samarraie et al., "Young Users' Social Media Addiction: Causes, Consequences and Preventions," Emerald Insight, November 18, 2021. www.emerald.com.

In 2019 researchers at Texas State University conducted a study involving 1,314 US adults aged eighteen to eighty-two to see whether there was any connection between social media overuse and generalized anxiety disorder (GAD). The researchers asked the respondents about their social media activity. They also gave the participants a well-known patient health questionnaire designed to assess the presence of GAD. The researchers found that "participants with GAD had significantly higher addiction scores than those without GAD."[35]

A review of the scientific literature by researchers at the University of Derby in the United Kingdom found that problematic social networking site use (PSNSU) was associated with other psychiatric disorders in all nine studies that fit the group's review criteria. The researchers determined that there is an association between PSNSU and depression (seven studies), anxiety (six studies), stress (two studies), ADHD (one study), and obsessive-compulsive disorder (one study). "Overall, the studies reviewed showed associations between PSNSU and psychiatric disorder symptoms, particularly in adolescents," write the researchers. "Most associations were found between PSNSU, depression, and anxiety."[36] While it is possible that excessive social media use is contributing to the psychiatric disorders, it is more likely that people—especially young people—who already have psychiatric disorders are using social media to modify their moods. It is these underlying psychiatric conditions that are driving their social media overuse, not an actual addiction to the technology.

> "Overall, the studies reviewed showed associations between [problematic social networking site use] and psychiatric disorder symptoms, particularly in adolescents."[36]
>
> —Researchers at the University of Derby in the United Kingdom

A Lack of Addictive Behavior

A 2021 study by researchers at the University of Strathclyde in Scotland strongly suggests that social media overuse is not really an addiction. The Scottish study is one of the first to directly test for addictive behavior in social media users. The researchers designed an experiment to measure a behavior known as attention bias, which is a hallmark of both substance abuse and behavioral addictions. Researchers have found that when addicted individuals are presented with an image related to their addiction, they respond differently than people who are not addicted. The former experience a release of dopamine in the part of the brain that governs goal-directed behavior. "Moreover," the researchers explain, "once users' attention is inordinately captured by addiction related content, they appear to show a significantly higher degree of 'cue reactivity,' leading to a greater craving for, and propensity to engage in, the addictive behaviour."[37]

The Scottish researchers showed the social media users simulated cell phone screens with various logos for apps, including social media apps. The researchers asked the participants to locate specific social media apps as quickly as possible. They also asked the participants questions about their social media use. The study found no correlation between performance in the logo-finding test and social media overuse. "We did not find evidence of attentional bias," write the researchers. "People who frequently checked and posted their social media accounts were no more likely to have their attention drawn to the icon of a social media app than those who check and post less often. . . . Our research indicates that frequent social media use may not, at present, necessarily fit into traditional addiction frameworks."[38]

So far, science has failed to show that social media overuse is a real addiction, complete with symptoms like withdrawal and relapse. When such symptoms exist, it is often among social media users with underlying mental health conditions. Saying that someone is addicted to social media—or believing it about oneself—is a way of escaping responsibility for a behavior that can be controlled, even if it is difficult to do. It suggests that people have less power over their lives than they really do—a belief that can keep people from taking responsibility for their actions.

> "Our research indicates that frequent social media use may not, at present, necessarily fit into traditional addiction frameworks."[38]
>
> —Researchers at the University of Strathclyde in Scotland

Source Notes

Overview: A Challenge to Civil Society

1. Quoted in Vivek Saxena, "'Extreme' Buffalo Gunman Threatened HS Graduation Shooting, Referred for 'Mental Health Eval,'" BPR, May 15, 2022. www.bizpacreview.com.
2. Quoted in White House, "Remarks by President Biden and First Lady Biden Honoring the Lives Lost in Buffalo, New York, and Calling on All Americans to Condemn White Supremacy," May 17, 2022. www.whitehouse.gov.
3. Quoted in Rebecca Hersher, "What Happened When Dylann Roof Asked Google for Information About Race?," NPR, January 10, 2017. www.npr.org.
4. Quoted in Flora Carmichael and Jack Goodman, "Vaccine Rumours Debunked: Microchips, 'Altered DNA' and More," BBC, December 2, 2020. www.bbc.com.
5. Quoted in Janna Anderson and Lee Rainie, "The Future of Truth and Misinformation Online," Pew Research Center, October 19, 2017. www.pewresearch.org.

Chapter One: Is Social Media Use Harmful to Youth Mental Health?

6. Quoted in McLean Hospital, "The Social Dilemma: Social Media and Your Mental Health," January 21, 2022. www.mcleanhospital.org.
7. Quoted in Alex Hern, "Instagram Is Supposed to Be Friendly. So Why Is It Making People So Miserable?," *The Guardian* (Manchester, UK), September 17, 2018. ww.theguardian.com.
8. Quoted in Royal Society for Public Health, "Instagram Ranked Worst for Young People's Mental Health," May 19, 2017. www.rsph.org.uk.
9. Quoted in Georgia Wells, Jeff Horvitz, and Deepa Seetharaman, "Facebook Knows Instagram Is Toxic for Teen Girls, Company Documents Show," *Wall Street Journal*, September 14, 2021. www.wsj.com.
10. Quoted in Hern, "Instagram Is Supposed to Be Friendly."
11. Quoted in Wells, Horvitz, and Seetharaman, "Facebook Knows Instagram Is Toxic for Teen Girls, Company Documents Show."

12. Quoted in Monica Greep, "Teenager, 17, Who Simply 'Liked' Some Sad Quotes on Instagram Reveals How the Site's Algorithm Sucked Her into Suicide Groups—and Admits It Made Her Believe Self-Harm Was 'Glamorous,'" MailOnline, February 7, 2022. www.dailymail.co.uk.
13. Quoted in Greep, "Teenager, 17, Who Simply 'Liked' Some Sad Quotes on Instagram Reveals How the Site's Algorithm Sucked Her into Suicide Groups."
14. Vivek Murthy, *Protecting Youth Mental Health: The U.S. Surgeon General's Advisory*. Washington, DC: US Department of Health and Human Services, 2021, p. 4.
15. Facebook, *Teen Mental Health Deep Dive*, 2019. https://about.fb.com.
16. Anya Kamenetz, "Facebook's Own Data Is Not as Conclusive as You Think About Teens and Mental Health," NPR, October 6, 2021. www.npr.org.
17. Quoted in Kamenetz, "Facebook's Own Data Is Not as Conclusive as You Think About Teens and Mental Health."
18. Victoria Rideout et al., "Fact Sheet: The Coronavirus, Depression, and Social Media Use Among U.S. Teens and Young Adults," Common Sense Media, 2021. www.commonsensemedia.org.

Chapter Two: Should Social Media Companies Regulate Speech?

19. Quoted in Maria Cramer, "Texas Man Is Sentenced to 15 Months for Online COVID-19 Hoax," *New York Times*, October 6, 2021. www.nytimes.com.
20. Quoted in Cramer, "Texas Man Is Sentenced to 15 Months for Online COVID-19 Hoax."
21. Quoted in Richard Gray, "Lies, Propaganda and Fake News: A Challenge for Our Age," BBC, March 1, 2017. www.bbc.com.
22. Quoted in Keith Zubrow, "Facebook Whistleblower Says Company Incentivizes 'Angry, Polarizing, Divisive Content,'" CBS News, October 4, 2021. www.cbsnews.com.
23. Quoted in Zubrow, "Facebook Whistleblower Says Company Incentivizes 'Angry, Polarizing, Divisive Content.'"
24. John Milton, "John Milton *Areopagitica*, 1644," First Amendment Watch, November 27, 2017. https://firstamendmentwatch.org.
25. *New York Times Co. v. Sullivan*, 376 U.S. 254 (1964).

Chapter Three: Is Social Media Addictive?

26. Javfly33, "Heavily Addicted to Scrolling and Refreshing Social Media/YouTube/the Forum . . . Etc," Actualized.org, January 31, 2021. www.actualized.org.
27. Quoted in Simon Parkin, "Has Dopamine Got Us Hooked on Tech?," *The Guardian* (US edition), March 4, 2018. www.theguardian.com.
28. Quoted in Parkin, "Has Dopamine Got Us Hooked on Tech?"
29. Quoted in Erin Bunch, "You Can Officially Hide Likes on Instagram—Here's Why Psychologists Say That's Good for Mental Health," Well + Good, April 28, 2021. www.wellandgood.com.
30. Quoted in Chloe Metzger, "I'm in Love with Myself: The Age of Digital Narcissism," *Marie Claire*, February 12, 2018. www.marieclaire.com.
31. Quoted in Hilary Andersson, "Social Media Apps Are 'Deliberately' Addictive to Users," BBC News, July 4, 2018. www.bbc.com.
32. Andrew K. Przybylski et al., "Motivational, Emotional, and Behavioral Correlates of Fear of Missing Out," *Computers in Human Behavior*, July 4, 2013. www.sciencedirect.com.
33. Chrissa Hardy, "I'm Addicted to Social Media & It's Ruining My Life," Bolde, February 24, 2017. www.bolde.com.
34. Quoted in Megan Teske, "Iowa State Research Shows That Some May Be at More Risk for Video Game Addiction," *Iowa State Daily* (Ames, IA), November 6, 2018. www.iowastatedaily.com.
35. Aaron Bonnette et al., "Upward Social Comparisons and Posting Under the Influence: Investigating Social Media Behaviors of U.S. Adults with Generalized Anxiety Disorder," *Spotlight on Mental Health Research*, October 2019. https://digital.library.txstate.edu.
36. Zaheer Hussain and Mark Griffiths, "Problematic Social Networking Site Use and Comorbid Psychiatric Disorders: A Systematic Review of Recent Large-Scale Studies," *Frontiers in Psychiatry*, 2018. www.ncbi.nlm.nih.gov.
37. Katie Thomson et al., "Social Media 'Addiction': The Absence of an Attentional Bias to Social Media Stimuli," *Journal of Behavioral Addiction*, July 2021. www.ncbi.nlm.nih.gov.
38. Thomson et al., "Social Media 'Addiction.'"

Social Media Facts

Social Media Usage

- More than 4.7 billion people—about 59 percent of the world's population—are social media users, according to the report *Digital in 2022: Global Overview* by We Are Social and Hootsuite.
- The number of social media users increased by 5.1 percent from July 2021 to July 2022, an increase of 227 million new users in one year, according to We Are Social and Hootsuite.
- Seven new users join social media platforms every second, according to We Are Social and Hootsuite.
- Eighty-two percent of the population in the United States has a social networking profile, according to Statista.
- Ninety-one percent of social media users access the platforms via mobile devices, according to We Are Social and Hootsuite.

Social Media Content Data

- YouTube users watch 4,146,600 videos every minute of the day, according to business intelligence firm Domo's *Data Never Sleeps 5.0* report.
- Instagram users post more than 67 million photos every day, according to Domo.
- Facebook users upload more than 300 million photos per day, according to Zephoria, a digital marketing firm.
- Facebook users post 510,000 comments every minute, according to Zephoria.
- More than 40 billion photos and videos have been shared on the Instagram platform since its conception, according to company data.

Social Media Platforms

- Facebook is the world's largest social media platform, with 2.9 billion monthly active users, according to Kepios, a consulting firm specializing in digital behavior.
- YouTube has 2.6 billion monthly active users, according to Statista.
- Instagram has 2 billion monthly active users worldwide, according to Statista.
- WhatsApp is the world's most popular mobile messenger app, with approximately 2 billion monthly active users, according to Statista.
- TikTok has 1 billion monthly active users, according to company data.

Related Organizations and Websites

Common Sense Media

www.commonsensemedia.org

Common Sense Media is an independent nonprofit organization that provides education, ratings, and tools to families to promote safe technology and media for children and teens. Its goal is to help kids thrive in a world of media and technology.

FactCheck.org

www.factcheck.org

FactCheck.org is a nonprofit website with the self-described mission of reducing the level of deception and confusion in US politics. The website features a Viral Spiral section devoted to debunking social media misinformation.

Get Net Wise

www.getnetwise.org

Get Net Wise is a website supported by internet industry corporations and public interest organizations. Its goal is to ensure that internet users have safe and constructive online experiences. The website contains information about digital citizenship, media literacy, and online misinformation.

Internet & Technology

www.pewinternet.org

Through its Internet & Technology website, the Pew Research Center studies how Americans use the internet and how digital technologies are shaping the world today. Its website has the results of numerous studies about social media and the internet.

National Cyber Security Alliance

www.staysafeonline.org

This website offers educational materials, information for home users on protecting their computers and their children, cybersecurity practices, videos, a self-assessment quiz, and additional resources.

Snopes

www.snopes.com

Founded in 1994, Snopes is the oldest and largest fact-checking website. Its easily searchable database allows users to see what the Snopes investigators have learned about various social media posts and other online stories. Its fact-check articles often include links to documenting sources so readers can do independent research and make up their own minds.

For Further Research

Books

Mark Carrier, *From Smartphones to Social Media: How Technology Affects Our Brains and Behavior*. Santa Barbara, CA: Greenwood, 2018.

Jill Keppeler, *Fake News*. New York: Rosen Young Adult, 2020.

Jaron Lanier, *Ten Arguments for Deleting Your Social Media Accounts Right Now*. New York: Henry Holt, 2018.

Bradley Steffens, *The Dark Side of Social Media*. San Diego: ReferencePoint, 2021.

Bradley Steffens, *Screen Addiction*. San Diego: ReferencePoint, 2022.

Susan Wroble, *Online Addiction*. San Diego: Brightpoint, 2022.

Internet Sources

Brooke Auxier, "64% of Americans Say Social Media Have a Mostly Negative Effect on the Way Things Are Going in the U.S. Today," Pew Research Center, October 15, 2020. www.pewinternet.org.

Institute of Humane Studies, "Social Media, Tribalism, and the Prevalence of Fake News," *Big Think* (blog), June 12, 2019. https://theihs.org.

Anya Kamenetz, "Facebook's Own Data Is Not as Conclusive as You Think About Teens and Mental Health," NPR, October 6, 2021. www.npr.org.

Kate Linebaugh, "The Facebook Files, Part 2: 'We Make Body Image Issues Worse,'" *The Journal* (podcast), *Wall Street Journal*, September 14, 2021. www.wsj.com.

Moya Lothian-McLean, "My Beautiful Dark Twisted Phone-tasy: 10 Long Years of Phone Addiction," *gal-dem*, March 5, 2021. https://gal-dem.com.

Jean Twenge, "The Facebook Expose: Four Things Parents Need to Know," Institute for Family Studies, October 11, 2021. https://ifstudies.org.

Georgia Wells, Jeff Horvitz, and Deepa Settharaman, "Facebook Knows Instagram Is Toxic for Teen Girls, Company Documents Show," *Wall Street Journal*, September 14, 2021. www.wsj.com.

Index

Note: Boldface page numbers indicate illustrations.

Actualized.org, 39
addiction, to social media
  as behavioral addiction, 41–43
  brain chemistry and, 40–41
  fear of missing out and, 43
  is not recognized as addiction, 44–45
  potential numbers suffering from, **42**
American Psychiatric Association (APA), 44–45
Areopagitica (Milton), 35
attention bias, 48–49

behavioral addiction, 41–43
Biden, Hunter, 32–33
Biden, Jill, **8**
Biden, Joe, 7, **8**, 32, 33
black salve, 9
Brennan, William, 36
Bruck, David, 7
Buterin, Vitalik, 28–29

Camus, Renaud, 7
Cascio, Jamais, 26
Combs, Christopher, 27

Common Sense Media, 10, 23–24, 46, 55
Constitution, US. *See* First Amendment; Nineteenth Amendment
COVID-19 pandemic, disinformation and, 9, 26–27, 30
Cramer, Shirley, 15
Crusius, Patrick, 7

depression, 15, 23, 46, 48
Diagnostic and Statistical Manual of Mental Disorders (DSM-5), 45, 46
dopamine, 40, 41
Dorsey, Jack, 11

EarthWeb (website), 18
eating disorders, 16, 17
Ehrlich, Joshua, 39
El Paso Walmart shooting (2019), 7
England, censorship in, 35
ETH (cryptocurrency), 28–29
Eyal, Nir, 44

Facebook (social media site), 10
  efforts to combat misinformation, 30

factors in overuse of, **47**
FactCheck.org (website), 55
fear of missing out (FOMO), 43
First Amendment, 35–36

Galilei, Galileo, 35
Gates, Bill, 9–10
Gendron, Payton, 6–7
generalized anxiety disorder (GAD), 47–48
Gentile, Douglas, 43
Get Net Wise (website), 55
Griffiths, Mark D., 42–43
Guarda, Angela, 13, 16

Hardy, Chrissa, 43
Haugen, Frances, 15, 17, 19, 20, 30–31

imposter syndrome, 13
Influencer Marketing Hub, 42
Instagram (photo-sharing app), 10
  factors in overuse of, **47**
  impact on self-image, 13–14, **14**, 16
  percentage of US teens using, 18
Internet & Technology (website), 55
internet gaming disorder (IGD), 45

Kamenetz, Anya, 20, 22

Lawson, Helen, 9
Le Grand Remplacement (Camus), 6–7
Lewandowsky, Stephan, 29

mass shootings, 6, 7–8
McDade, Niamh, 16
McLaughlin, John, 33
medical disinformation, 9–10
mental health, of youth
  debate over social media as harmful to, 12
  social media has negative impact on, 13–15
  social media overuse and, 46–48
Milton, John, 35
misinformation
  cost of, 28–29
  medical, 9–10
  social media companies need to do more to police, 29–31
  social media efforts to remove, 11, 30
Murthy, Vivek, 17–18
Musk, Elon, 32

National Cyber Security Alliance (website), 56
NewsGuard, 28
New York Post (newspaper), 32–34

New York Times Co. v. Sullivan (1964), 36
Nineteenth Amendment, 36

Obama, Barack, 4, 32
Odgers, Candice, 23
online harassment, 30
　prevalence of, 8–9
opinion polls. *See* surveys
Ordinance for the Regulating of Printing (England, 1643), 35

Perez, Christopher Charles, 26–27
Pew Research Center, 8–9, 10, 11, **34**
Pietsch, Lena, 30
polls. *See* surveys
problematic social networking site use (PSNSU), 48

Raskin, Aza, 41
Rideout, Victoria, 19
Roof, Dylan, 7
Royal Society for Public Health (RSPH), 15

Schüll, Natasha, 40
Schultz, Wolfram, 40
self-image, Instagram impact on, 13–14, **14**, 16
Snopes (website), 55

social media
　debate over addictive nature of, 38
　dopamine-triggering features of, 40–41
　factors in overuse of, **47**
　as harmful to youth mental health, debate over, 12
　has negative impact on youths' mental health, 13–15
　interactions on, by source credibility, **28**
　numbers potentially suffering from addiction to, **42**
　positive effects of, 23–24
　self-harm linked to, 17–18
　use to spread terror, 27
　See also addiction, to social media
social media companies
　Americans' trust in, to censor data, **34**
　efforts to remove misinformation, 11, 30
　First Amendment not applicable to, 36
　need to do more to police misinformation, 29–31
　role in regulating speech, debate over, 25
South Carolina church shooting (2015), 7
Statista, 31

61

Stone, Andy, 32–33
suicide, 20, 24
surveys
  on depression and social media, 23–24
  on impact of Instagram on various experiences, **21**
  on impact of social media, 10
  on Instagram impact on self-image, 13–14, **14**, 16
  on prevalence of online harassment, 8–9
  on prevalence of use of social media, 10
  on trust in social media companies to censor data, **34**
  on use of Instagram among US youth, 18

Technology In Society (journal), 42

Thomson, Katie, 49
Tops supermarket shooting (Buffalo, NY, 2022), 6–7
Twitter (social media site), 11
  efforts to combat misinformation, 30
  factors in overuse of, **47**

University of Derby, 48
University of Essex, 43
University of Strathclyde, 48

vaccines, misinformation about, 9
Vogel, Erin A., 41

Washington Post (newspaper), 33
White replacement theory, 6–7

Zuckerberg, Mark, 11

Picture Credits

Cover: Maridav/Shutterstock.com

8: White House Photo/Alamy Stock Photo
14: Maury Aaseng
21: Maury Aaseng
28: Maury Aaseng
34: Maury Aaseng
42: Maury Aaseng
47: Maury Aaseng

About the Author

Bradley Steffens is a novelist, poet, and award-winning author of more than sixty nonfiction books for children and young adults.